NATIONAL GEOGRAPHIC

Common Core Readers

Ladders

High Points

Up High

Land and water cover Earth. The largest landmasses on Earth are called **continents.** There are seven continents. Some people think mountains are the most amazing places on land. It is a test for a **mountaineer** to climb the highest mountains. The highest mountains are the Seven **Summits.** These are the highest mountains on each continent.

The Seven Summits + 1

MOUNT McKINLEY or DENALI

Alaska, United States
20,320 feet (6,194 meters)

Mountaineers and many others call this mountain *Denali*. That means "The High One" in the Athabaska language. Others call it *Mount McKinley*.

MOUNT ACONCAGUA

Argentina
22,834 feet (6,959 meters)

Aconcagua is part of the Andes Mountains, the world's longest mountain range. Its name might be from the words *Ackon Cah*. They mean "Sentinel of Stone" in the Quechua language.

VINSON MASSIF

Antarctica
16,050 feet (4,892 meters)

This peak was discovered in 1935. It was first climbed in 1966. By 2012, about 1000 climbers had tackled it. Most do so in November through January, which is summer in Antarctica.

NORTH AMERICA

SOUTH AMERICA

ATLANTIC OCEAN

PACIFIC OCEAN

MOUNT ELBRUS

Russia
18,510 feet (5,642 meters)

Mount Elbrus is part of the Caucasus Mountains. Together with the Ural Mountains, they form the border between Europe and Asia.

KILIMANJARO

Tanzania
19,340 feet (5,896 meters)

Kilimanjaro is an extinct volcano. Mountaineers can take different routes to its summit. The climate varies from route to route. Snow and ice cover some parts.

MOUNT EVEREST

Nepal and China (Tibet)
29,035 feet (8,850 meters)

Mount Everest has a higher **elevation** than any other mountain in the world. One side of the mountain is in Nepal. The other side is in China (Tibet).

CARSTENSZ PYRAMID

Indonesia
16,024 feet (4,884 meters)

According to most mountaineers, Carstensz Pyramid is part of Australia/ Oceania. So mountaineers list this peak as the seventh summit, not Mount Kosciuszko.

ARCTIC OCEAN

EUROPE

ASIA

AFRICA

MOUNT KOSCIUSZKO

Australia
7,310 feet (2,228 meters)

For mountaineers, this peak is an easy climb. That's one reason many don't include it on their Seven Summits list. Instead, they climb Carstensz Pyramid.

AUSTRALIA
and OCEANIA

INDIAN
OCEAN

PACIFIC
OCEAN

ANTARCTICA

High Points in the U.S.

The place in each state with the highest elevation is the state's high point. A high point can be a huge mountain or a low hill. The 50 high points in the U.S. are listed here, from highest to lowest.

Highest point in each state

Vermont
Mt. Mansfield
4,393 ft (1,339 m)

Kentucky
Black Mountain
4,145 ft (1,263 m)

Kansas
Mt. Sunflower
4,039 ft (1,231 m)

South Carolina
Sassafras Mountain
3,564 ft (1,086 m)

North Dakota
White Butte
3,506 ft (1,069 m)

Massachusetts
Mt. Greylock
3,489 ft (1,063 m)

Maryland
Backbone Mountain
3,360 ft (1,024 m)

Pennsylvania
Mt. Davis
3,213 ft (979 m)

Arkansas
Mt. Magazine
2,753 ft (839 m)

Alabama
Cheaha Mountain
2,413 ft (735 m)

Connecticut
Mt. Frissell
2,380 ft (725 m)

Minnesota
Eagle Mountain
2,301 ft (701 m)

Michigan
Mt. Arvon
1,979 ft (603 m)

Alaska
Mt. McKinley/Denali
20,327 ft (6,196 m)

California
Mt. Whitney
14,505 ft (4,421 m)

Colorado
Mt. Elbert
14,440 ft (4,401 m)

Washington
Mt. Rainier
14,411 ft (4,392 m)

Wyoming
Gannett Peak
13,809 ft (4,209 m)

Hawaii
Mauna Kea
13,796 ft (4,205 m)

Utah
Kings Peak
13,528 ft (4,123 m)

New Mexico
Wheeler Peak
13,161 ft (4,011 m)

Nevada
Boundary Peak
13,147 ft (4,007 m)

Montana
Granite Peak
12,807 ft (3,904 m)

Idaho
Borah Peak
12,668 ft (3,861 m)

Arizona
Humphreys Peak
12,633 ft (3,851 m)

Oregon
Mt. Hood
11,249 ft (3,429 m)

Wisconsin
Timms Hill
1,951 ft (595 m)

New Jersey
High Point
1,803 ft (550 m)

Missouri
Taum Sauk Mtn.
1,772 ft (540 m)

Iowa
Hawkeye Point
1,670 ft (509 m)

Ohio
Campbell Hill
1,549 ft (472 m)

Indiana
Hoosier Hill
1,257 ft (383 m)

Illinois
Charles Mound
1,235 ft (376 m)

Rhode Island
Jerimoth Hill
812 ft (247 m)

Mississippi
Woodall Mountain
807 ft (246 m)

Louisiana
Driskill Mountain
535 ft (163 m)

Delaware
Ebright Azimuth
448 ft (137 m)

Florida
Britton Hill
345 ft (105 m)

Check In Which high point is nearest to you?

LOW HIGH POINTS
The high points in some states are very low! In fact, the Empire State Building has a higher elevation than some high points.

SEA LEVEL
If we say that a mountain is 535 feet high, we mean that it is 535 feet higher than **sea level**, or the level of the ocean.

Empire State Building
1,250 feet (381 meters)

Britton Hill, FL | **345 feet**

Ebright Azimuth, DE | **442 feet**

Driskell Mountain, LA | **535 feet**

Jerimoth Hil, RI | **812 feet**

Charles Mound, IL | **1,235 feet**

Sea level

Texas
Guadalupe Peak
8,751 ft (2,667 m)

South Dakota
Harney Peak
7,244 ft (2,208 m)

North Carolina
Mt. Mitchell
6,684 ft (2,037 m)

Tennessee
Clingmans Dome
6,643 ft (2,025 m)

New Hampshire
Mt. Washington
6,288 ft (1,917 m)

Virginia
Mt. Rogers
5,729 ft (1,746 m)

Nebraska
Panorama Point
5,424 ft (1,653 m)

New York
Mt. Marcy
5,344 ft (1,629 m)

Maine
Mt. Katahdin
5,270 ft (1,606 m)

Oklahoma
Black Mesa
4,973 ft (1,516 m)

West Virginia
Spruce Knob
4,863 ft (1,482 m)

Georgia
Brasstown Bald
4,784 ft (1,458 m)

THE 50 50 50 EXPEDITION

by Matt Moniz

"50 states, 50 high points, 50 days."

That's how 12-year-old Matt Moniz described his trip. He went with his dad Mike and a team of **mountaineers**. They started in May, 2010. Their goal was to go to each state. That's 50 states. Climb the highest point. That's 50 high points. And to do it in 50 days. This is Matt's account of the trip. It starts with the highest point, Denali.

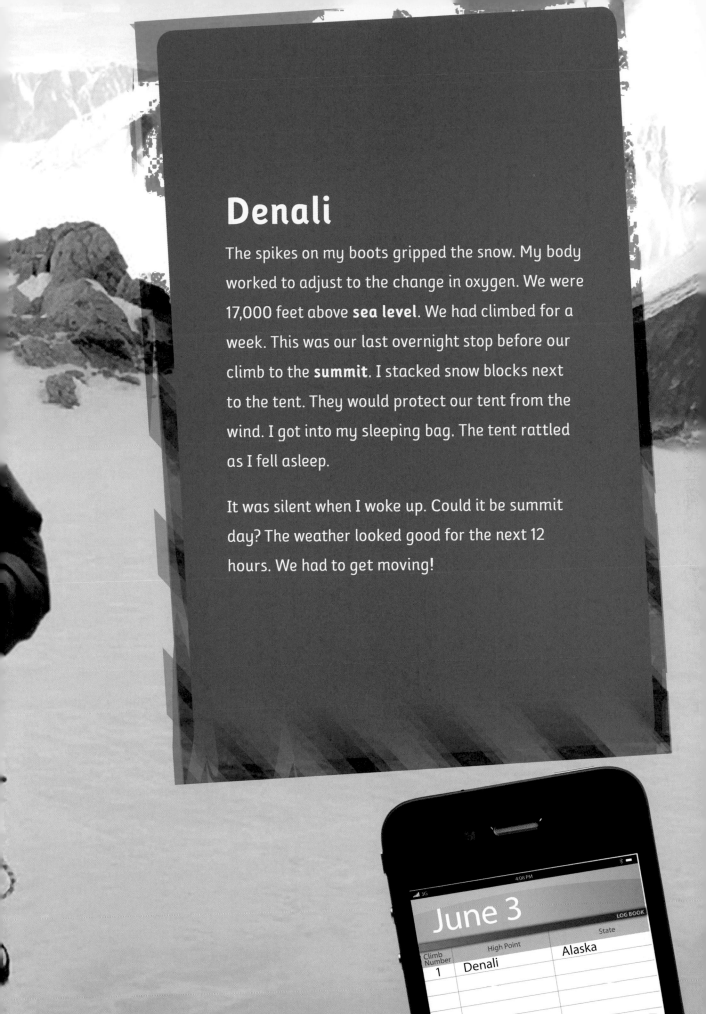

Denali

The spikes on my boots gripped the snow. My body worked to adjust to the change in oxygen. We were 17,000 feet above **sea level**. We had climbed for a week. This was our last overnight stop before our climb to the **summit**. I stacked snow blocks next to the tent. They would protect our tent from the wind. I got into my sleeping bag. The tent rattled as I fell asleep.

It was silent when I woke up. Could it be summit day? The weather looked good for the next 12 hours. We had to get moving!

4:08 PM

3G

June 3

LOG BOOK

Climb Number	High Point	State
1	Denali	Alaska

We used ropes to climb a difficult part of the mountain. I wore thick mittens. This made it hard to clip my hook onto the rope. It was warm and not too windy. But I saw clouds in the distance. This can mean the weather is getting worse.

Over the next few hours I climbed the highest land in North America.

"Almost there," I thought. Finally, we were on the path that led to the summit. I saw prayer flags ahead. We had reached the summit. I was standing at the tip of the United States. It was June 3, 2010, at 12:04 p.m. in Alaska. We had met our first goal!

This hook is called a carabiner. It's one of the many pieces of equipment used on the expedition.

Climbing the summit ridge of Denali, I knew the top was within reach!

Dad and I on the summit of Denali

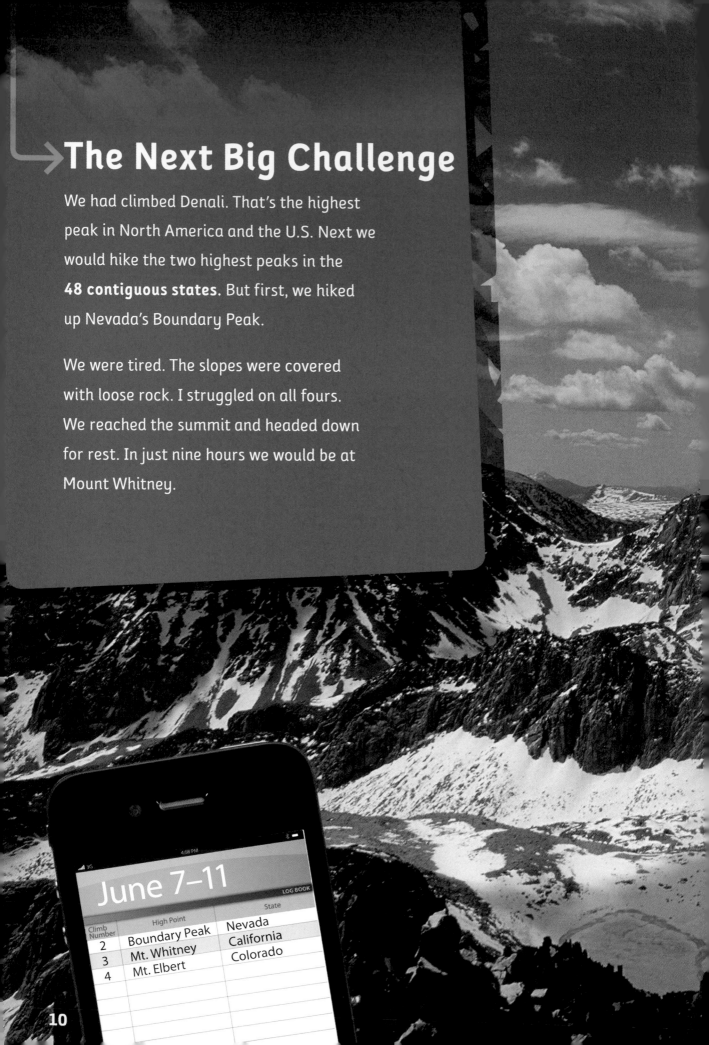

The Next Big Challenge

We had climbed Denali. That's the highest peak in North America and the U.S. Next we would hike the two highest peaks in the **48 contiguous states**. But first, we hiked up Nevada's Boundary Peak.

We were tired. The slopes were covered with loose rock. I struggled on all fours. We reached the summit and headed down for rest. In just nine hours we would be at Mount Whitney.

4:08 PM

3G

June 7–11

LOG BOOK

Climb Number	High Point	State
2	Boundary Peak	Nevada
3	Mt. Whitney	California
4	Mt. Elbert	Colorado

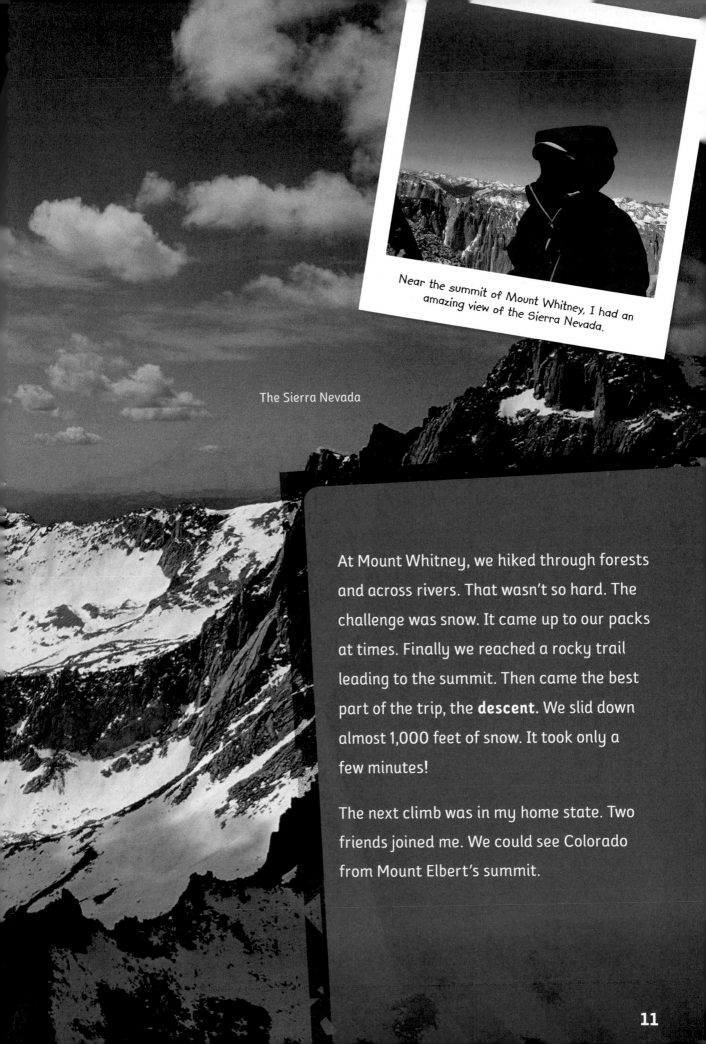

Near the summit of Mount Whitney, I had an amazing view of the Sierra Nevada.

The Sierra Nevada

At Mount Whitney, we hiked through forests and across rivers. That wasn't so hard. The challenge was snow. It came up to our packs at times. Finally we reached a rocky trail leading to the summit. Then came the best part of the trip, the **descent**. We slid down almost 1,000 feet of snow. It took only a few minutes!

The next climb was in my home state. Two friends joined me. We could see Colorado from Mount Elbert's summit.

Wonderland

We traveled through eight states over the next few days. First was New Mexico. We climbed Mount Wheeler. There were thunderstorms during the climb. The storm passed and we made it to the summit. We had climbed five peaks. Our next five were fairly easy.

Next, we drove from Black Mesa in Oklahoma through the Badlands of South Dakota. Then we went to White Butte in North Dakota. We climbed high points in Kansas and Nebraska on the way!

Friends hiked some high points close to my home state of Colorado. Here we are on Mount Wheeler, in New Mexico.

Black Mesa, Oklahoma

Team member Joel and I signed the guest book at Mount Sunflower, Kansas—in the dark!

We traveled by plane and van to Arizona and Texas. Humphreys Peak is a desert mountain in Arizona. There were lots of bugs at its summit. Then, we were on to the mountains of Guadalupe National Park, Texas. We saw a tree there with reddish bark. It was called the Texas madrone.

Texas madrone tree

June 12–15

LOG BOOK

Climb Number	High Point	State
5	Wheeler Peak	New Mexico
6	Black Mesa	Oklahoma
7	Mt. Sunflower	Kansas
8	Panorama Point	Nebraska
9	Harney Peak	South Dakota
10	White Butte	North Dakota
11	Humphreys Peak	Arizona
12	Guadalupe Peak	Texas

4:08 PM

Snow in the South

Louisiana's Driskill Mountain has an **elevation** of 535 feet. It was an easy climb. The hard part was the biting bugs! Next, we drove north into the Ozark Mountains of Arkansas and Missouri. After a hike to the top of Mount Magazine we stopped for breakfast.

We checked Missouri's high point off our list. Then we headed south. We neared Mount Woodall in Mississippi. I thought I saw snow, but it was moths. Lots of them. They made me think of the real snow I had seen a few weeks before.

A benchmark like this marks the summit of most high points. This benchmark is at the summit of Mount Magazine, Arkansas.

June 16–17

Climb Number	High Point	State
13	Driskill Mtn.	Louisiana
14	Mt. Magazine	Arkansas
15	Taum Sauk Mtn.	Missouri
16	Woodall Mtn.	Mississippi

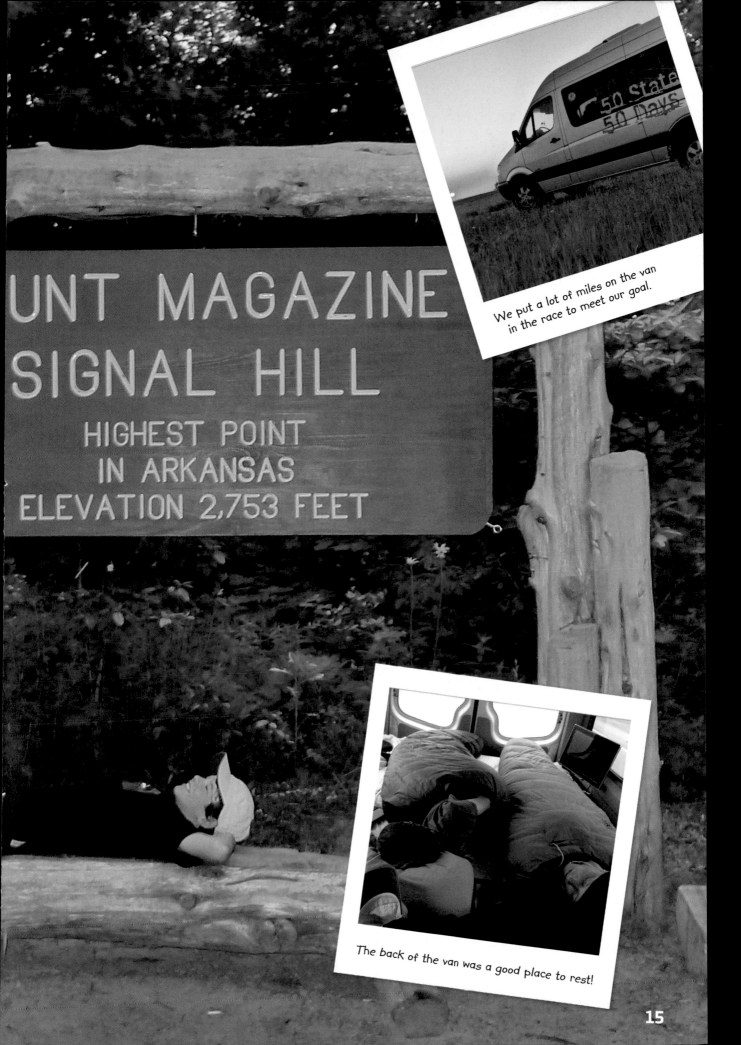

UNT MAGAZINE
SIGNAL HILL

HIGHEST POINT
IN ARKANSAS
ELEVATION 2,753 FEET

50 State
50 Days

We put a lot of miles on the van in the race to meet our goal.

The back of the van was a good place to rest!

A Whole Lotta States

The Appalachian Mountain Range goes from Alabama to Maine. The Appalachian Trail connects 14 states in the range. We would visit them all and more.

Some of the climbs were difficult. A stormy **ascent** of Mount Frissell in Connecticut was like climbing a river. A muddy approach made it hard to climb Mount Marcy in New York.

Mount Washington has extreme weather. The wind there almost blew me off the top!

On Mount Katahdin, I met a man who had just finished hiking the Appalachian Trail!

The photo on Katahdin shows part of our team. Team members on other parts of the trip included climbers Charley Mace (Mt. Everest, K2, Seven Summits) and Brian Stevens. It also included pilots John Shoffner and Russ Betcher, physician Dan Busse, MD, and many friends.

It was rain, rain, and more rain in the Northeast. Water gushed down the rocky trail on Mount Mansfield, in Vermont.

Team members from left to right: Ben Thomas (videographer), David Holmberg (climber), Joel Gratz (meteorologist), Mike Moniz (my dad), me

4:08 PM

June 18–26

LOG BOOK

Climb Number	High Point	State
17	Cheaha Mtn.	Alabama
18	Britton Hill	Florida
19	Brasstown Bald	Georgia
20	Sassafras Mtn.	South Carolina
21	Mt. Mitchell	North Carolina
22	Mt. Rogers	Virginia
23	Black Mtn.	Kentucky
24	Clingmans Dome	Tennessee
25	Spruce Knob	West Virginia
26	Backbone Mtn.	Maryland
27	Mt. Davis	Pennsylvania
28	Ebright Azimuth	Delaware
29	High Point	New Jersey
30	Mt. Frissell	Connecticut
31	Mt. Greylock	Massachusetts

4:08 PM

June 18–26

LOG BOOK

Climb Number	High Point	State
32	Mt. Marcy	New York
33	Mt. Mansfield	Vermont
34	Mt. Washington	New Hampshire
35	Mt. Katahdin	Maine
36	Jerimoth Hill	Rhode Island

Planes, Bikes, and More Hikes!

In the Great Lakes region, we got around by airplane. We landed in Illinois. Then we rode bikes to Charles Mound. The air was hot and sticky. I was glad to get to the high point and look at the view.

I liked our pattern of flying and climbing. I really enjoyed the flight from Michigan to Minnesota. I helped fly the airplane! From the cockpit, I could see north into Canada. I had been looking south into Mexico just ten days earlier.

Riding in the cockpit was exciting. It was a different kind of high point!

Ruffed grouse

Most treks in this area were easy, but Eagle Mountain was hard. The trail twists along lakes and bogs. We saw a bird called a ruffed grouse. It charged at me. I decided to go a different way!

Iowa's high point is decorated with a mosaic. Signs point to locations around the world.

4:08 PM

June 26–28

Climb Number	High Point	State
37	Charles Mound	Illinois
38	Timms Hill	Wisconsin
39	Mt. Arvon	Michigan
40	Eagle Mtn.	Minnesota
41	Hawkeye Point	Iowa
42	Hoosier Hill	Indiana
43	Campbell Hill	Ohio

LOG BOOK

Real Mountaineering

After the Midwest, it was back to real mountaineering. First was Mount Rainier in Washington. This is one of the most difficult U.S. high points. Rainier is 14,000 feet high. It has 26 glaciers. It is also an active volcano! After two difficult days we reached Rainier's crater rim. It was the final hurdle before the summit. "Yes!" I shouted at the top.

The second climb was Oregon's Mount Hood. From the top I could see Mount St. Helens, Mount Rainier, and Mount Adams.

I used a snowboard for a quick descent on Mount Hood.

Even on snowy Mount Rainier, it was cozy inside the tent.

Once in Utah, we had only five peaks left. Four of them would be difficult. We pulled up to the base of Kings Peak at 11 p.m. The main bridge was washed out. We hiked for three miles until we found a spot to cross the river. We hiked through the night. At 6 a.m. we stopped to rest.

I took a one-hour nap, but I was still tired. I got up anyway. At 11 a.m. we reached the top. Mosquitoes kept us moving quickly on the descent. We completed the 32-mile trip in about 20 hours!

Here I am, napping on the way to the summit of Kings Peak.

4:08 PM

3G

July 2–4

LOG BOOK

Climb Number	High Point	State
44	Mt. Rainier	Washington
45	Mt. Hood	Oregon
46	Kings Peak	Utah

The Grand Finale

In Wyoming, we had a long hike ahead of us. We went by horse part of the way. At the summit, my dad asked what peak we were on. "Number 57," I said. He laughed and said, "Since when are there 57 states?" I could tell I was getting tired.

Idaho's Borah Peak had steep cliffs covered with shale. The shale reminded me of a dragon's back. I was glad to finish this peak. Two more to go.

Granite Peak was next. But there was a problem. We had heard that it was covered in deep snow. Then strong winds ripped our tent. My dad called Joel, our weather expert. Joel said the storm would let up. Soon there wasn't a cloud in the Montana sky.

My climbing skills were tested that day. Only Denali was more difficult. "Forty-nine, YES!" I yelled from the peak.

It felt good to rest my legs and let Dora do the work!

"Matt, get up!" my sister Kaylee said. I was half asleep. "What mountain is next?" I asked. Then I remembered. WE DID IT! We were in Hawaii. Kaylee and my mom joined Dad and me the day before. We hiked to the 50th peak, Mauna Kea. We met our goal and set a record. We climbed all 50 peaks. We did it in 43 days, 3 hours, and 51 minutes!

We finally made it to peak number 50, Mauna Kea.

July 9–16

LOG BOOK

Climb Number	High Point	State
47	Gannett Peak	Wyoming
48	Borah Peak	Idaho
49	Granite Peak	Montana
50	Mauna Kea	Hawaii

Check In What challenges did Matt face while meeting his goal?

Kaylee's Account

written and illustrated by

I'm Kaylee, Matt's twin sister. I am a **freestyle skier.**
I have also climbed mountains, including Kilimanjaro. It
has the highest **elevation** in Africa. I have also climbed
fourteeners. Those are mountains with an elevation of
more than 14,000 feet above **sea level.**

Matt and I climbed Kilimanjaro when
we were 10. I hold the record for the
youngest female to reach its summit.

You read Matt's account of his trip. I did not go along. But I know a lot about it. This is my account of Matt's trip.

Matt's main goal was to reach the highest point in each state. Another goal was to make people aware of Pulmonary Arterial Hypertension, or PAH. It is a disease that affects his friend Iain. When Iain is active, he can feel short of breath. **Mountaineers** often feel the same way at high elevations.

Iain and Matt

Matt's first climb was Denali. It would be rugged and long. Matt would carry a backpack with 50 to 60 pounds of supplies. He would pull a sled with about 40 pounds of gear. Matt built up **endurance** by carrying a 50-pound backpack. It was filled with jugs of water.

One gallon of water weighs a little over 8 pounds. So wearing a 50-pound pack is like carrying about 6 gallons of water! (8 × 6 = 48)

My mom and I gave Matt a gift to take on the trip. It was light, and practical, too. It helped hold up his pants!

Our backyard is on the side of a mountain. Matt climbed it wearing the backpack. Sometimes he fell. He had a hard time getting up. We helped him out. Matt also jogged wearing the backpack. Sometimes friends and I joined him.

Eat, Sleep, Climb, Drive

Matt and Dad left for Denali in May. Matt and I texted about every other day. After climbing Mount Elbert, they got into a routine: eat, sleep, climb, drive. Then they'd do it all again!

I spent part of the summer at a camp in Wyoming. It rained a lot and even snowed. Matt and Dad were nearby, climbing Harney Peak in South Dakota. I thought they must be cold, too.

I planned to do some climbs with Matt and Dad, but their schedule was crazy. One example is Guadalupe Peak in Texas. They reached the **summit** at 5:54 a.m. They must have started climbing really early! But that was easy compared to Kings Peak in Utah. They climbed all night long there.

Phew!

I found out that I would do one of the climbs after all. I would climb the last point, Mauna Kea. When I saw Matt, he looked a little different than before. His hair was longer. Some of his skin was sunburned. He acted different, too. He was nicer to me.

Mom took the picture. Matt, Dad, and I said "cheese!"

Mauna Kea wasn't too hard to climb. It was more like a hike than a climb.

The trip was over when we got to the summit of Mauna Kea. Matt and Dad had hiked over 300 miles. They also flew in planes, drove in a van, and rode bikes and horses. They had done it all in 43 days. No wonder Matt was tired. Phew!

Check In What thoughts and observations did Kaylee have about the expedition?

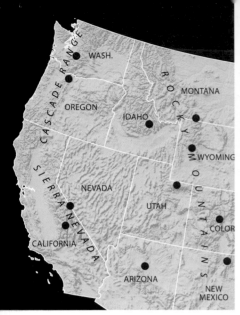

Discuss | Compare and Integrate Information

1. How did the map and the other information in "Up High" help you understand the other two pieces in this book? Explain.

2. Choose a high point. Write what you learned about it from "Up High" and "The 50-50-50 Expedition." Tell the information to a partner.

3. How is Matt's firsthand account organized? Compare this to the organization of Kaylee's secondhand account. How are the accounts alike and different?

4. What information does Kaylee include in her secondhand account that Matt does not include in his firsthand account?

5. What do you still wonder about the 50-50-50 Expedition?